CRITICAL WORLD ISSUES

Racism

Critical World Issues

CRITICAL WORLD ISSUES

Racism

Chuck Robinson

MASON CREST
PHILADELPHIA

Mason Crest
450 Parkway Drive, Suite D
Broomall, PA 19008
www.masoncrest.com

Printed and bound in the United States of America.

CPSIA Compliance Information: Batch #CWI2016.
For further information, contact Mason Crest at 1-866-MCP-Book.

First printing
1 3 5 7 9 8 6 4 2

Library of Congress Cataloging-in-Publication Data

on file at the Library of Congress
ISBN: 978-1-4222-3659-8 (hc)
ISBN: 978-1-4222-8139-0 (ebook)

Critical World Issues series ISBN: 978-1-4222-3645-1

Table of Contents

KEY ICONS TO LOOK FOR:

Words to Understand: These words with their easy-to-understand definitions will increase the reader's understanding of the text, while building vocabulary skills.

Sidebars: This boxed material within the main text allows readers to build knowledge, gain insights, explore possibilities, and broaden their perspectives by weaving together additional information to provide realistic and holistic perspectives.

Research Projects: Readers are pointed toward areas of further inquiry connected to each chapter. Suggestions are provided for projects that encourage deeper research and analysis.

Text-Dependent Questions: These questions send the reader back to the text for more careful attention to the evidence presented there.

Series Glossary of Key Terms: This back-of-the book glossary contains terminology used throughout this series. Words found here increase the reader's ability to read and comprehend higher-level books and articles in this field.

What Is Racism?

E rrol, a seventeen-year-old black American, experienced racism while living in several parts of the United States. "I always remember name-calling and monkey signs made at me and the other black kids out of class," he said. "My mother told me not to let it get to me. 'To react back makes you as low as they,' she told me and I tried, but it still made me feel bad about myself, like I wasn't as good as them.

"When we moved west, I went from being one of many black kids to the only one in the neighborhood. People, parents, kids, old people—they all used to stare at me. Several times, folks told me stores were closed even when I could see others inside buying things. When I went into stores, I was followed

Errol, an African-American teenager, experienced racism while living in a rural part of the United States. As one of the relatively few black people living in the area, he was made to feel different from other people.

around by clerks, like I was gonna steal something. I thought it funny the first time. But it happened all the time.

"School was bad there. I tried to make friends but one kid, Ryan, got beaten up by older white kids for hanging out with me and stopped. My grades got worse. Some of the teachers started to pick on me for making noise in class, even when it couldn't be me—I had no one to talk to. My locker was broken into and "Nigger thief" written inside, but I hadn't stolen anything.

"I don't want to say much about the worst thing that happened. Some white men I didn't know grabbed me one night and tied me up. They hit my legs with a metal pipe over and over again. I needed three operations on my right leg. At the time, I thought I was going to die.

"We moved to New York soon after I got out of the hospital. I hear about lots of crime here but I feel much safer, like I'm

---

 Words to Understand in This Chapter

culture—the traditions, values, lifestyles, and beliefs shared by a group of people.

ethnic group—a group of people who share the same distinct culture, religion, way of life or language.

genetics—the scientific study of human characteristics passed down through generations via genes.

Hispanic—Spanish-speaking people living in the United States whose families originally came from Latin America.

nationalism—a belief that a person's nation is superior to others.

xenophobia—a fear and hatred of foreigners.

Errol has had a better experience since moving to a suburb of New York with a supportive community.

not the one guy everyone wants to hate anymore. I still don't understand how you hate people who are strangers you know nothing about. I still have nightmares about what happened. 1 never want to be like them."

What Is Racism?

There are more than seven billion people living on Earth. They live in more than 200 countries, with thousands of different beliefs and *cultures*. Some people believe that human beings can be separated into distinct groups. They believe these

Most people have come to understand that the concept of "race" is meaningless. It falsely implies that there are significant genetic differences between populations.

groups, or races, are biologically different from each other and can be identified through skin color, facial appearance, and what they believe to be a set of innate characteristics and skills.

Racists use this idea to label certain races as fundamentally different and inferior.

Some people celebrate the differences between peoples because they add richness and diversity to life. Others use certain differences to single out certain groups as inferior and deserving of unfair treatment. Racism is one such way to single people out who are different. It has caused misery and suffering for millions.

Racism is based on the flawed belief that a person's character and abilities can be determined by their physical characteristics, and that certain racial groups are inferior to others. To determine which racial group a person belongs to, racist people

Marchers rally against racism after the shooting death of a young African American named Michael Brown in Ferguson, Missouri.

look purely at a person's physical appearance, not at what sort of personality, interests, or beliefs they have. Racism doesn't focus on all aspects of physical appearance but mainly on skin color and, sometimes, certain facial features.

People who believe in racism are called racists. Racists generally believe that members of their own race, or racial group, are superior to other groups. The "higher race" is seen as more creative, intelligent and morally stronger. Other "lesser races" are considered not to be trustworthy, well-behaved, hardworking, or bright. As a result, racists feel justified in treating members of other groups as inferiors.

This idea of superior and inferior racial groups has been used as an excuse for the most horrific actions, from preventing another race from gaining equal education or employment opportunities, to beatings, murders, and even attempts to wipe out entire races of people.

How Many Races Are There?

One of the founders of race theory, the Frenchman Count Joseph-Arthur Gobineau (1816–1882), believed there were three races—white, black, and yellow. Others divided the world's population into as many as thirty different races. In all cases, these races were seen as completely different species or sub-species of human beings.

Science has since shown there is just one species of people, to which we all belong, and that people of all colors and appearances have similar potential. In 1945, the United Nations Economic, Scientific and Cultural Organization (UNESCO) stated that "available scientific evidence provides no basis for

One of the many thousands of happy mixed race families in the United Kingdom.

believing that the groups of mankind differ in their innate capacity for intellectual and emotional development."

Modern research into *genetics* has revealed how people differ from one another. Around 30,000 genes control a person's physical characteristics. These create the great variety of shapes, sizes, and looks that make the world's seven billion people different from one another. Yet only around six genes control all the differences in skin color. This means that people of different skin colors might have far more genes in common

Research into human DNA and genetics has helped to disprove the notion that there are different biological races.

than people with the same skin color do. There are no distinct sets of "black" or "white" or "Asian" or "*Hispanic*" genes. The idea of different biological races of people is false.

Despite the notion of race being proven wrong by science, race remains a huge issue. This is because many people still believe in the idea of widely different races and because many societies continue to give "racial" differences a great amount of significance.

Non-Racial Group Distinctions

The term *racism* is sometimes widely used and applied to any group that attacks or discriminates against another group. However, although racists use physical characteristics to distinguish between different peoples, there are other ways in which groups can be singled out. Some people define themselves and others by the religions they hold: for example, as Christians, Muslims, Jews, or Hindus. Rather than embracing and respecting a range of beliefs, they may act against peoples who follow other religions. Other people are *nationalists* who take pride in their country to extremes, believing their nation to be superior and peoples of other countries inferior. Being *xenophobic* (hating and fearing foreign peoples) or intolerant of other religions like Judaism or Islam, is not the same as racism, although these attitudes can be just as harmful.

Ethnicity is not the same as race either, although the two terms are often used interchangeably. Ethnicity relates to the the cultural beliefs and lifestyle of a particular group of people that set them apart from others. Different things can distinguish a particular *ethnic group*. They commonly include

Members of a large Hispanic family celebrate a birthday. Hispanics are considered an ethnic group, rather than a racial group.

language, history, religion, and styles of dress. Ethnic differences are learned, whereas a person is born with the color of his or her skin. A person who is considered racially Asian due to their skin color and physical features can also be classified as being of Japanese, Vietnamese, Pakistani, or Chinese ethnicity.

Victims of Racism

Racism's direct victims are mainly non-white people, but white anti-racism campaigners are frequently the victims of racist

action. People in mixed black and white families may be singled out by racists for "betraying their own race." In some
places, merely having a friend of another race has been enough
for a person to receive hate mail, letter-bombs, or bricks
through home windows. Racism in an area can create a climate
of mistrust and fear, which can envelop everyone who lives
there, not just the racists and their direct victims.

 ## Text-Dependent Questions

1. Who was one of the founders of race theory?
2. What is the difference between race and ethnicity?
3. Approximately how many genes control a person's physical characteristics?

 ## Research Project

Using the Internet or your school library, do some research to answer the question, "Do
different beliefs equal different peoples?" Some people will contend that if people believe
in different things and live in different ways, then surely they are different. Others will
argue that ethnic differences such as beliefs, dress, and diet are not a biological part of a
person. People from one ethnic group can learn and practice the ways of other ethnic
groups. Present your conclusion in a two-page report, providing examples from your
research that support your answer.

The Origins of Racism

*D*iscrimination is as old as humankind, and throughout history, people of different clans, tribes, nationalities, or groups have fought with each other for control of resources or territory. In the ancient and medieval worlds, people apparently did not regard skin color as any more significant than any other physical characteristic, such as height, hair color, or eye color. Tomb paintings from ancient Egypt show what looks like random mixtures of white-skinned, brown-skinned, and black-skinned figures. In early sixteenth-century Dutch paintings, people with white and black skins are portrayed side by side as equals.

The skin color–based racism that is described in this book apparently had its roots in the age of European colonialism, which began more than 500 years ago. As Europeans discov-

The first cargo of African-American slaves are landed at the English colony of Jamestown, Virginia, in 1619. Slavery was already widespread in other European settlements in South America, Central America, and the Caribbean.

ered and claimed overseas lands as colonies, the belief grew that European civilization was the greatest the world had ever known. Europeans thus felt justified in treating other peoples as inferior.

From the sixteenth century onwards, many European countries like France, Portugal, Spain, Holland, and Great Britain explored and claimed lands in Africa, Asia, the Americas, and the Pacific as their own. Little attempt was made by the arriving colonists to understand the civilization, culture, and beliefs of the native peoples. Instead, they were often thought of as savage primitives, or in some cases as wild

 Words to Understand in This Chapter

anti-Semitism—hatred of the Jewish people.

apartheid—literally meaning "apartness," the political policies of the South African government from 1948 until 1990, which were designed to keep people segregated based on their color.

boycott—the cutting of relations with a country, company or group of people by removing trade, cultural and government links.

colony—a country ruled by another country as part of its empire.

discrimination—the act of treating people worse because they belong to a particular group.

genocide—the deliberate attempt to kill all of the members of a racial, ethnic or religious group.

persecute—to harass, ill-treat, injure or kill a particular group of people.

segregation—the separation of different racial groups as far as possible in everyday life.

slavery—a system where one group of people own another group as their property and force them to work.

During the sixteenth century, the conquest of indigenous peoples by Hernan Cortes and other Spanish conquistadores enabled Europeans to establish colonies in Central and South America. Large farms, called plantations, were created for the Spanish colonists. To work the farms, the Spaniards first turned to the Native Americans. When they died out, they began to import slave laborers from Africa.

animals. As a result, the colonists assumed the right to take their lands, ruling them without their agreement, and killing or mistreating millions of people, while turning millions more into *slaves.*

The African Slave Trade

Colonial settlement in the Caribbean and South America by the Spanish and Portuguese marked the beginning of a triangular trade network in which European slave ships took people from Africa to the Caribbean and the Americas and brought back

Slaves were captured in African tribes in battle and sold to Arab traders, who marched them to the coast where they could be sold to Europeans for the transatlantic slave trade.

New World products to Europe.

As early as 1482 the Portuguese began to establish numerous trading posts along the coast of West Africa, where they built castles that served as holding stations for slaves being sent overseas. In 1518, the year that King Charles I of Spain authorized the slave trade from Africa to the New World, the first shipment of African-born slaves arrived in the West Indies, as the Caribbean islands were known.

Portugal maintained its monopoly on the slave trade in Africa until the 16th century, when England, followed by

France and other European nations, entered the profitable business. The rapidly growing demand for sugar and tobacco that began during the 17th century fueled the demand for slave labor, resulting in a significant increase in the triangular slave trade.

Between 1500 and 1888, millions of Africans were captured and shipped out of the continent. Estimates of the total number of enslaved Africans vary widely. Conservative estimates contained in Angus Maddison's *The World Economy: Historical Statistics* put the number of black African slaves exported to the

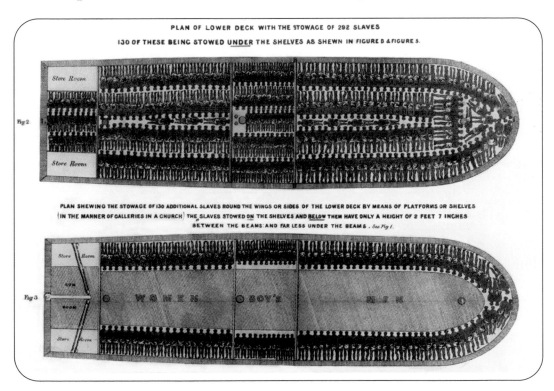

This illustration shows how slaves were crowded onto ships. Chained together in cramped, unsanitary conditions, with inadequate food and water, millions of Africans died on the journey across the Atlantic to the English, Spanish, and Portuguese colonies in the Americas.

Americas during this time at just over 11 million. Other historians estimate the number to be 15 million or more. During the same period, another 3.2 million black Africans were taken across the Sahara to serve as slaves in Europe and almost 2 million more were kidnapped and sent to Asia.

The actual number of African lives lost as a result of the slave trade was far greater than the amount sold into slavery. The toll includes the many people who perished in slave-generating wars and conflicts, as well as those who died during the long, brutal passage to their final destination.

At the time the transatlantic slave trade took place, there was little understanding of the concept of universal human rights, including the right to life and liberty. In Africa, people lived in societies in which their loyalty lay with their extended family and community, so the idea of capturing and enslaving members of another community, especially one that was a rival for limited resources (such as land or water), did not seem immoral. Whites, also, justified their actions by drawing on ancient Greek and Roman writings that permitted the enslavement of those captured during war.

Evolving Concept of Race

The idea of race was originally used to describe a person's family background—who their ancestors were, for example. It was also sometimes used when talking about the country a person lived in or the religion they practiced, with phrases such as the "the Jewish race" or "the French are the finest race."

As slavery became essential to the European colonial enterprise, eighteenth-century societies adapted the concept of racial

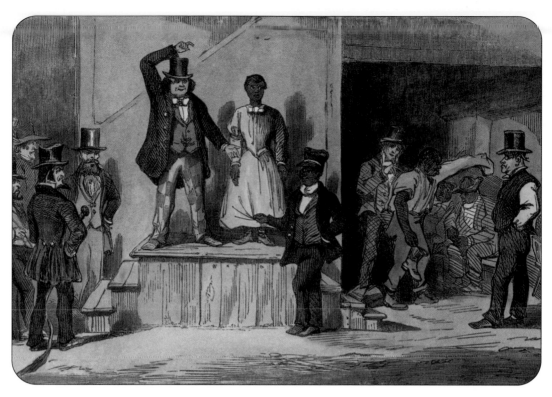

View of a black woman slave being auctioned in Virginia, 1856. Whites justified slavery by promoting the belief that black people were inferior—a lower class of humans.

differences in order to justify their actions. Most white Europeans were Christians, so they turned to the Bible to find an excuse for slavery. Christian supporters of slavery developed a theory that Africans were descended from Ham, the cursed son of Noah. According to this theory, God didn't care if Africans were enslaved—in fact, He approved.

Others, who took a more scientific view, determined that Africans were "sub-human." The influential Scottish philosopher and historian David Hume (1711–1776), expressed this attitude when he noted, "I am apt to suspect the Negroes, and

Although they have lived in Australia for over 50,000 years, Aborigines were only granted full citizenship rights in 1967. Before 1971, anyone considered more than half Aboriginal was not counted as part of the national population.

in general, all other species of men, to be naturally inferior to the whites. There never was any civilized nation of any other compaction [complexion] than white." This meant the great thinkers of the century could proclaim that "all men are created equal," and still condone slavery, since non-whites were not men. Racism based on color was now born.

Also during the eighteenth century, an idea developed that all people were of one single type of fixed race—black, white, yellow, etc.—which could never change. Mixed-race people were thought of as unnatural—exceptions in nature that would die out quickly. Often, mixing of the races through relationships was frowned upon or forbidden.

Racial *segregation* was not unique to the United States. In many countries, European colonial leaders imposed systems where they separated white colonists from the colored people who lived in the countries. In Australia and New Zealand, the aboriginal people were nearly wiped out by British settlers. In the Congo territory of Africa, which was a Belgian *colony*, white rule was particularly oppressive and dehumanizing for Africans. Natives were forced to work on large plantations or be killed. The Germans were also harsh colonial masters in their southwest African colonies. The German government attempted to exterminate the indigenous Herero and Nama peoples after they revolted in 1904, killing more than 80 percent of their populations. And in British India, the native Hindu people did not have the same rights and privileges as the relatively few white colonial settlers of the region.

During the nineteenth century, the naturalist Charles Darwin wrote about the idea of evolution and how different species of creatures change over time, adapting to the conditions where they live. Instead of exploding the myth of unchanging racial differences, parts of Darwin's work were used by some people to promote and justify the idea that white Europeans were superior to all others. For example, some took Darwin's concept of "survival of the fittest" and maintained that because the white race was the most technologically advanced, it was appropriate for Europeans to exploit other, less advanced races. Others took Darwin's idea of evolution to maintain that they could measure skulls and other physical features to place all races in a line back to humanity's "monkey ancestors." According to this incorrect theory, white peoples were the most evolved and advanced, while black peoples were the least evolved and therefore closest to the monkeys.

These ideas were held by many people in the Western world until the mid-twentieth century, when science showed that distinct species of humans do not exist and the world learned about Nazi Germany's attempt at *genocide*, the deliberate killing of an entire group of people.

Anti-Semitism in Europe

Anti-Semitism is the hatred of Jews, which has led to Jews being *persecuted* for their beliefs in different countries for many centuries. There is no such thing as a Jewish race—Judaism is a religion—but in Nazi Germany (1933-45), the Jewish people were treated as a race. Under the leadership of Adolf Hitler, the Nazis believed in permanent racial types with the white German, or Aryan, race being supreme and the Jews cast as the biggest threat to Aryan supremacy. The Jewish Untermenschen (meaning "subhumans"), were first harassed and then persecuted ruthlessly. By 1941, the Nazis' attempt to exterminate all Jewish people was under way. By the end of World War II, four years later, six million of Europe's eight million Jews had been murdered.

A world shocked at the Nazi genocide formed the United Nations in 1945 with the aim "to save succeeding generations from the scourge of war." Although racism continued to exist, it became more and more discredited as a way of acting publicly.

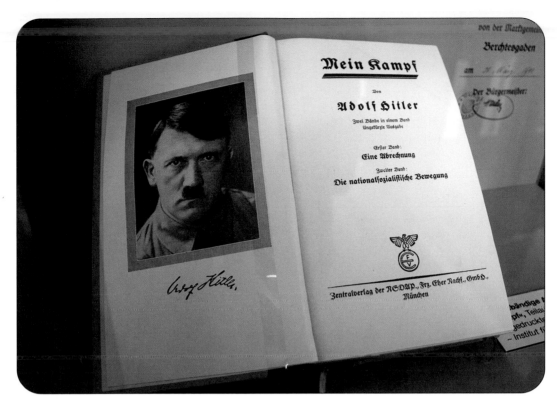

In Mein Kampf *("My Struggle"), published in 1925, Adolf Hitler maintained that it was the Nazi Party's duty "to promote the victory of the better and stronger [races] and demand the subordination of the inferior and weaker."*

Apartheid in South Africa

Despite the changing views, in some countries racial segregation became national policy. This was the case in South Africa, which in 1948, under the leadership of Dr. Daniel E Malan, introduced an official policy called *apartheid* ("apartness"). Malan explained the program by saying, "Apartheid is a way of saving the white civilization from vanishing beneath the black sea of south Africa's non-European populations."

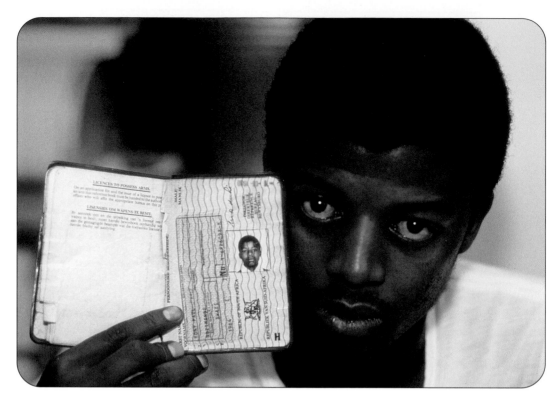

A black South African shows his government-issued passbook. Under the apartheid system in South Africa, blacks are required to carry passes that determined where they may live.

South Africa was already a racially divided country with laws separating blacks from whites before 1948. However, the apartheid laws forced everyone suspected of not being of European origin to be classified by race. Every aspect of life in South Africa was segregated by race. There was whites-only public transport, leisure facilities, beaches and even park benches. The Mixed Marriages Act made it illegal to marry someone of a different race, while the Group Areas Act forced people of certain races to live in specific areas. Many black people were forced to live in townships outside major cities or in "homelands" in rural areas. In these designated areas the farm-land, schooling, healthcare, and job opportunities were extremely poor. Many blacks were forced to work for white employers with their pay, conditions and rights vastly inferior to those of white workers.

Movement between areas, as well as civil rights for the blacks and Coloureds (as those of Indian or biracial descent were known) were strictly controlled by the authorities. Laws gave the police and military sweeping powers to put down any resistance to the apartheid regime. On many occasions, the white authorities acted brutally. In 1960 a demonstration

Segregated bus stops for black and white passengers in Johannesburg.

Nelson Mandela (seated) signs the oath of office as he assumes the presidency of South Africa on May 10, 1994.

against apartheid in the black township of Sharpeville resulted in the police opening fire, killing 69 men, women and children and injuring over 180 more. Resistance to apartheid also came from outside South Africa with protests, condemnation by the United Nations, sanctions and *boycotts*. Sanctions banned certain economic trade occurring between South Africa and other countries. Boycotts prevented South Africa from taking part in many international sporting and cultural events.

Due in part to these pressures, in 1990 South African president Frederik Willem de Klerk initiated policies to end apartheid. That same year, black social activist and political leader Nelson Mandela was freed after 27 years in prison for rebelling against the government. Mandela became the first black president of South Africa in 1994 and formed a multi-ethnic government that transitioned the country out of apartheid and toward equality. Mandela and de Klerk were jointly awarded the 1993 Nobel Peace Prize "for their work for the peaceful termination of the apartheid regime, and for laying the foundations for a new democratic South Africa."

 # Text-Dependent Questions

1. How were the ideas of Charles Darwin applied to the concept of racial differences?
2. What was the apartheid system?

 # Research Project

Using the Internet or your school library, do some research to answer the question, "Is affirmative action a good idea?" Supporters of affirmative action tend to believe that these programs and policies help to compensate for wrongs against members of minority groups that were committed in the past. They also note that, since the mid-1960s, many qualified members of minority groups have benefited from affirmative action policies. Opponents of affirmative action view these policies as a form of discrimination that is unfair to white people who had nothing to do with the racist policies of the past. They feel that affirmative action leads to resentment and antagonism in the majority population. Offering everyone an equal chance of success, in their view, is the only fair policy. Present your conclusion in a two-page report, providing examples from your research that support your answer.

3

Fighting Racism in the United States

The American tradition of government places great emphasis on the importance of civil rights. Yet the nation has been far from perfect in living up to its ideals. Throughout much of American history, black people were prevented from exercising the same rights and enjoying the same privileges as others. During the period in which slavery existed in North America, from around 1619 until 1865, enslaved African Americans had no rights. They couldn't be citizens. Under the law, they were property. The children of slaves also became property. Slave owners had the legal right to do almost anything they wished with their slaves.

Even after slavery ended, African Americans continued to suffer unfair treatment. In the South, a web of laws and social rules was put in place to prevent blacks from becoming equal

A masked Ku Klux Klan member holds a noose outside a car window during a parade through an African-American neighborhood in Florida on the night before an election, May 1939. Groups like the Ku Klux Klan used violence and intimidation to prevent blacks from enjoying all the rights of citizenship.

This nineteenth century sheet music includes offensive stereotypes of African Americans singing and dancing. The name Jim Crow came from a popular song, but was eventually applied to laws that kept blacks as second-class citizens.

members of society. This system of racial discrimination was known as Jim Crow. In many states, laws required racial segregation—the separation of blacks and whites—in public places. These laws prevented black people from using the same public facilities as whites. For example, blacks weren't allowed to stay in hotels where whites stayed. They couldn't get served in restaurants where whites ate. They had to ride on "colored only" train cars. They could not even drink from the same drinking fountains. Black children had to go to separate schools. In almost every case, the facilities set aside for African Americans were inferior to those used by whites.

 ## Words to Understand in This Chapter

Jim Crow—a term for southern laws created after the Reconstruction period, which restricted the rights of African Americans.

lynching—the execution of an accused person by a mob outside of the law.

A US Supreme Court ruling in 1896 supported the practice of segregation. In a case known as *Plessy v. Ferguson*, the Court determined that African Americans were not entitled to use the same public facilities as whites, so long as they were provided with public facilities that were similar to the ones whites used. "Separate but equal" treatment of the races, the Court said, was perfectly legal.

At the same time, Southern states also established rules that made it impossible for most African Americans to vote. This effectively stopped the black community from changing Jim Crow through the political process. Jim Crow was also preserved through informal means. Black people who challenged the system faced the threat of violence from their white neighbors. And violence against African Americans was rarely punished when committed by whites.

Until the 1960s, many southern states had laws that required segregation of whites and blacks. This cafe in Durham, North Carolina, has separate entrances and seating areas for white and black patrons.

Conditions for African Americans were worst in the South. But racial segregation existed in other parts of the country as well. And for many decades the federal government did nothing to address the injustices.

By the early 1900s, Jim Crow was thoroughly entrenched in the South. African-American leaders disagreed on what course to take. Some were willing to accept segregation, at least in the short term. The black community, they said, should concentrate on self-improvement through hard work and education. Equality under the law would come eventually. The most famous advocate of this viewpoint was the educator Booker T. Washington.

Other black leaders demanded that African Americans receive full civil rights immediately. W. E. B. Du Bois was per-

Juvenile convicts at work in the fields in a chain gang, circa 1903. Southern jails made money leasing convicts for forced labor in the Jim Crow South.

This black man was one of thousands lynched in the South between the 1890s and the 1920s. Black people were sometimes lynched when accused of a crime; however, in some cases blacks were lynched just for talking back to whites. In the West, other minority groups, such as Hispanics or Chinese immigrants, were also targeted by lynch mobs.

haps the most influential champion of this position. Born in Massachusetts in 1868, Du Bois became the first African American to receive a doctoral degree from Harvard University. He wrote widely about racism and, in 1905, helped found an organization called the Niagara Movement. It brought together leading African-American intellectuals, writers, and journalists. The Niagara Movement had limited influence. Its membership never grew to more than a few hundred.

But Du Bois helped found a much more significant civil rights organization. In August 1908, a deadly race riot tore through Abraham Lincoln's hometown of Springfield, Illinois. Shocked by the violence, about 60 concerned citizens met in New York City the following February. Du Bois was one of seven African Americans in attendance. The meeting led to the formation of the National Association for the Advancement of Colored People (NAACP). Its members were determined to see all Americans enjoy equal protection under the law.

The NAACP took a multi-pronged approach to the struggle for equality. Du Bois launched and was the longtime editor of the organization's magazine, called *The Crisis*. In its pages, talented writers chronicled the evils of racism and made the case for civil rights. The NAACP undertook a campaign against *lynching*. It organized protests against a popular 1915 motion picture, *The Birth of a Nation*, which glorified the Ku Klux Klan. The NAACP also mounted legal challenges to racist laws.

In 1940, the NAACP Legal Defense Fund was founded. Headed by a young African-American lawyer named Thurgood Marshall, the Legal Defense Fund would fight segregation in the courts.

Integrating the Military

Meanwhile, the struggle for civil rights was being waged in other arenas as well. In 1941, A. Philip Randolph, leader of a black labor union called the Brotherhood of Sleeping Car Porters, planned a 100,000-person march on Washington, D.C. Its purpose was to protest racial segregation in the American armed forces and discriminatory hiring practices in the defense industry.

To avert the huge demonstration, President Franklin D. Roosevelt signed Executive Order 8802. Issued on June 25, 1941, it prohibited employment discrimination in the defense industry. Roosevelt's executive order didn't address the other issue in question—segregation in the armed forces. Still, Randolph believed that progress had been made. He called off the protest march. The armed forces remained segregated.

During World War II—which the United States entered in December 1941 and which lasted until August 1945—African Americans served in segregated units. In many other ways, they were treated poorly. In 1947, Randolph and fellow activist Grant Reynolds decided to change the situation. They founded an organization dedicated to ending segregation in the U.S. military.

In June 1948, after the group was renamed the League for Non-Violent Civil Disobedience Against Military Segregation, Randolph brought matters to a head. He informed President Harry S. Truman that blacks would refuse to be drafted into the military unless the armed forces were integrated.

On July 26, 1948, Truman signed Executive Order 9981. "It is hereby declared to be the policy of the President," the order stated, "that there shall be equality of treatment and opportunity for all persons in the armed services without regard to race, color, religion, or national origin." Randolph and his colleagues had helped end racial segregation in the military. That victory would provide momentum for the growing civil rights movement.

School Desegregation

During the 1930s the NAACP began working to end the "separate but equal" doctrine established by *Plessy v. Ferguson*. The NAACP Legal Defense Fund filed lawsuits demanding that the educational facilities provided for black students be made equal to those for whites. Some of these suits proved successful. The overall goal of the NAACP was to end legal segregation altogether.

In December 1952 there were five school segregation lawsuits awaiting review by the U.S. Supreme Court. They represented more than 150 plaintiffs who were from several different states. All challenged the lawfulness of racial segregation practices in the public school system. The Court consolidated all five cases under one name: *Oliver Brown et al. v. the Board of Education of Topeka, Kansas*.

NAACP attorneys, including Thurgood Marshall, presented their arguments in *Brown v. Board of Education* on December 9, 1952. The lawyers argued that school segregation violated the "equal protection clause" of the Fourteenth Amendment to the US Constitution. This clause prohibits states from denying citizens equal treatment under the law. To support their case, the lawyers presented evidence that segre-

Attorneys George E. C. Hayes (left), Thurgood Marshall (center), and James M. Nabrit (right) celebrate outside the U.S. Supreme Court building after the Court ruled in May 1954 that school segregation was unconstitutional.

gated schools had a negative impact on African American students. The schools caused black children to believe they were not equal to whites. Segregation laws in education resulted in a separate and unequal education for black children.

The Supreme Court heard the case again on two more occasions. In May 1954 it submitted its decision. The Court agreed that segregation in public education violated the equal protection clause of the Fourteenth Amendment. In announcing the unanimous decision, Chief Justice Earl Warren wrote, "Segregation of white and colored children in public schools has a detrimental effect upon the colored children. The impact is greater when it has the sanction of the law. . . . We conclude that, in the field of public education, the doctrine of "separate but equal" has no place. Separate educational facilities are inherently unequal."

The Supreme Court ruled that racially segregated public schools were a violation of the U.S. Constitution. All public schools were ordered to desegregate.

The Civil Rights Movement Begins

The *Brown v. Board of Education* decision gave the civil rights movement a defining victory. However, the process of desegregating schools would take determination and time. The order to integrate public schools met with heavy resistance from Southern whites. It wasn't uncommon for resolute segregationists to refuse to integrate their public schools. Opposition came from public schools all over the South, from Texas and Kentucky to Tennessee and Mississippi.

Resistance took many forms. Rather than integrate, some white-dominated school boards closed schools. In other cases, mobs of angry whites prevented African American students from attempting to enter all-white schools. Some government officials openly opposed integration. They refused to enforce the ruling. It would be many years before public schools in the United States were integrated.

Montgomery Bus Boycott

Brown v. Board of Education only ended segregation in schools. It did not end segregation in other public areas. There were still whites-only restaurants, movie theaters, and restrooms. Many states and cities had laws that punished businesses that did not provide separate facilities for black and white customers. Some state laws prohibited interracial marriages. Others imposed segregation practices in public transportation.

In Montgomery, Alabama, city law required passengers on buses to be segregated. Whites took seats in the front rows. African Americans had to take seats in the back of the bus. If the bus became full, all the blacks in the row nearest the white section had to get up from their seats. This would create a new row for white passengers. If there were no seats available for them, African American riders were supposed to stand. In addition, black passengers often had to board the bus in the front door to pay the fare. But then they had to exit the bus and reenter using the rear door.

NAACP lawyers continued to challenge segregation in the courts. But in the 1950s, African Americans also used a tactic called civil disobedience to draw attention to the civil rights cause.

 # Nonviolent Resistance

Civil disobedience occurs when a person refuses to obey laws that the person feels are unfair. A key element of this tactic is that the person cannot fight back or resist the consequence of breaking the law, such as being thrown in jail. This is known as "nonviolent resistance," or nonviolence. The idea behind nonviolent civil disobedience is that when large groups of people allow themselves to be punished for refusing to accept unjust laws, their action draws public attention to the unfair situation. As the government realizes that people would rather go to prison than live under the existing laws and conditions, it is pressured to make changes.

The most famous act of American civil disobedience occurred on December 1, 1955. It involved 42-year-old Rosa Parks, who was leaving work when she got onto a Montgomery bus. Parks sat down in the first row of the bus's "colored" section—the seats from the middle to the back. After passengers filled all the seats, a white man was left standing. Another black man sat by Parks, in the window seat. Two black women sat across the aisle from Parks. The bus driver, James F. Blake, told the four black riders, "Let me have those seats." No one moved. Blake said "Y'all better make it light on yourselves and let me have those seats."

The man and two women stood. But Parks scooted into the window seat. In her autobiography *My Story* she said, "I could not see how standing up was going to 'make it light' on me. The more we gave in, [the worse they treated us]." Montgomery police officers boarded the bus and arrested Parks.

Within a few hours of Rosa Parks's arrest, Jo Ann Robinson heard the news. Robinson, an English professor at the all-black Alabama State College in Montgomery, was president of the Women's Political Council (WPC), a civil rights group of 300 women. For years, the WPC and other groups had talked about boycotting Montgomery's buses. In 1953, Robinson had sent a letter to the mayor of Montgomery, William Gayle, warning that African Americans would stop riding the buses if the abuses didn't stop. Robinson knew that African-Americans riders were important to the bus company. Three-quarters of the bus passengers were black, and if they stopped riding the bus company would lose a lot of money.

Early in the morning of December 2, 1955, Robinson and

Rosa Parks is fingerprinted after being arrested in December 1955.

three helpers met at Alabama State College. They printed 52,000 flyers on the college's mimeograph (copying) machine. The flyers told African Americans about Rosa Parks's arrest, and that her trial was scheduled for Monday, December 5. "Please stay off all buses Monday," read the flyers. WPC members posted flyers everywhere. The Sunday issue of the *Montgomery Advertiser*, a newspaper for the city's African-

American community, reproduced Robinson's message on the front page.

On December 5, Parks walked up the steps to the courthouse with E.D. Nixon, the head of the local NAACP chapter, and her lawyers Fred Gray and Charles Langford. About 500 supporters lined the steps as she passed. In court, the judge fined Parks $10 for disorderly conduct, plus $4 in court costs. That day, some 40,000 African Americans walked or found alternate ways to get to school or work. They refused to ride the Montgomery buses.

The bus boycott was so successful that local leaders decided to continue it. On the afternoon of December 5 a group called the Montgomery Improvement Association (MIA) was formed. They chose a Baptist minister who was new in town to lead the group: 26-year-old Martin Luther King Jr.

Over the next year, tens of thousands of African Americans—mostly women who worked as housekeepers, babysitters, and cooks—boycotted the Montgomery city buses. They walked or rode bicycles, mules, and horses. To get to work each day, about 30,000 boycotters rode in carpools. Some of the cars were driven by white women.

King and other MIA leaders, such as Nixon and the Reverend Ralph Abernathy, told the Montgomery Bus Company the boycott would continue until the company agreed to treat African American riders with respect, allowed them to sit wherever they wanted, and hired more black drivers.

The Montgomery Bus Company lost a significant amount of money without black riders. Plus, businesses in Montgomery suffered also, because African Americans refused to ride buses to shop. But the black community suffered too. Some people who supported the boycott were fired from their jobs by white bosses. Sometimes blacks walking to work were threatened or attacked. Police stopped black carpool drivers and gave them tickets for minor traffic violations. People set off bombs at the homes of King and Nixon. King and other leaders were also arrested. Still, the boycott continued.

The Montgomery bus boycott officially ended after 381 days, on December 20, 1956. By this time, the US Supreme Court had ruled that Alabama's segregation laws were unconstitutional. The success of the Montgomery bus boycott was a critical point in the history of the civil rights movement, and helped make Martin Luther King Jr. and others who had been involved in the boycott into nationally known figures. Most importantly, the success of the bus boycott showed blacks that by working together, they could bring about change.

Violence in Alabama

Many white people in the South refused to accept that times were changing. Their attitudes were summed up by Alabama governor George Wallace, who in January 1963 declared that he would continue to oppose efforts by the federal government to force integration of public facilities in Alabama. Wallace's statement "I say segregation now, segregation tomorrow, segregation forever" would become a rallying cry for those opposed to African American civil rights.

Birmingham, Alabama, was one of the most segregated cities in America, and violence against African Americans was so common that the city had been nicknamed "Bombingham."

Civil rights leaders began to boycott white-owned businesses and hold protest marches in the city. Black protesters were met with force. Firemen battered them with high-pressure streams of water from fire hoses. Law enforcement officers set police dogs on crowds. Police pummeled individuals with clubs. Photographs and television footage of the attacks on peaceful protesters horrified most of the country.

President John F. Kennedy urged local government officials to meet with protest leaders. On May 10, 1963, Birmingham officials freed thousands of student prisoners. The officials promised to racially integrate public places, make sure African American job-seekers got fair treatment, and continue meeting with African-Americans to address their concerns. A month later, Kennedy gave a televised speech to the nation. He called for federal laws that would ensure that all Americans, regardless of color, received equal treatment under the law.

March on Washington

Later in 1963, civil rights activists began planning a march on the U.S. capital, Washington, D.C. They wanted to send a message that African Americans deserved fair treatment. The event was called the "March on Washington for Jobs and Freedom."

On August 28, 1963, more than 250,000 people marched from the Washington Monument to the Lincoln Memorial. At the steps of the Memorial, they listened to opera star Marian Anderson and gospel singer Mahalia Jackson. They heard several men, representing various civil rights organizations, give speeches. The one that would be best remembered was delivered by King. That day he gave his famous "I Have a Dream" speech, in which he spoke about his desire for peaceful integration.

King's dream of peaceful integration seemed far off, however, as the violence resistance to integration continued throughout 1963. On September 15, 1963, four members of the Ku Klux Klan set off a bomb at the 16th Street Baptist Church in Birmingham, where King and others had planned the Birmingham campaign in the spring. Four young girls—11-year-old Denise McNair and 14-year-olds Addie Mae Collins, Carole Robertson, and Cynthia Wesley—were killed and 22 others were injured. It was the 27th bombing in Birmingham that year. The bombers would not be brought to justice for decades.

Freedom Summer

A year after the March on Washington, a civil rights organization called the Student Nonviolent Coordinating Committee began a major effort to register black voters in the South. At the time, many Southern blacks were still denied the right to vote. This was particularly true in Mississippi. The state had the lowest African American voter registration in the country. In 1962, less than 7 percent of eligible black voters were registered.

If you lived in Mississippi in 1964 and you were black, it was not easy to vote. First you had to register at the courthouse. You had to fill out a long form with 20 questions. You had to copy any section of the state's constitution. Then you had to explain what it meant—in writing. Many blacks in Mississippi

The Rev. Martin Luther King speaks to a crowd of about 250,000 people during the March on Washington for Jobs and Freedom, August 1963.

were poor and uneducated. Most of them couldn't qualify to vote. Because they weren't permitted to vote, African Americans could not decide who would represent them in the local, state, and national government. They could not elect African Americans or those who would work to end segregation and ensure civil rights for blacks.

SNCC decided to try to change that. Their project, called Freedom Summer, had many goals. The top goal was to help more blacks in Mississippi register to vote. Other goals were to open community centers, help black kids with reading and math, and start a new political party that would listen to the needs of African Americans.

College students from around the country—both black and white—volunteered to take part in the project. After a training session, the first group headed for Mississippi. Not long after that, three volunteers—Michael Schwerner, Andy Goodman, and James Chaney—disappeared. Their bodies were found buried together almost two months later. They had been murdered.

Those murders, and others, frightened other volunteers. During Freedom Summer, six people were murdered, 35 shootings were reported, at least 80 volunteers were beaten, and over 1,000 people were arrested. More than 60 churches, homes, or black-owned businesses were bombed or burned. But the violent attacks didn't stop the activists.

The Freedom Summer program didn't achieve all its goals, but it would make a big difference in the lives of African Americans in Mississippi. By 1969, the number of registered black voters had risen to more than 66 percent.

Civil Rights Legislation passes

In the summer of 1963 President Kennedy had proposed civil rights legislation, but he did not live to see it passed by Congress. After Kennedy's assassination in November 1963, his successor, President Lyndon B. Johnson, made sure that the proposed bill would become law.

The Civil Rights Act of 1964, which Johnson signed on July 2, outlawed discrimination based on an individual's race, color, religion, sex, or national origin. The Act outlawed segregation in businesses such as theaters, restaurants, and hotels. It banned discriminatory practices in hiring, promoting, setting wages, and firing employees. And it outlawed segregation in public facilities such as swimming pools, libraries, and public schools.

The Civil Rights Act was a major step, but it was not enough. Activists wanted another federal law that would ensure voting rights for African Americans. Public support for this law increased after police brutally broke up a voting rights march in Alabama. On March 7, 1965, 600 civil rights protesters began a march from Selma to the state capital of Montgomery. They were attacked with billy clubs and tear gas. The day became known as Bloody Sunday.

On March 21, around 3,000 marchers led by Martin Luther King Jr., set out again. This time, participants in the Selma to Montgomery march were escorted by the Alabama National Guard. On March 25, when the marchers reached the state capital, they numbered 25,000.

The news media reported on the voting rights march. And there was growing public support to remove obstacles that pre-

President Lyndon B. Johnson signs the 1965 Voting Rights Act. Watching are many civil rights leaders, including Dr. Martin Luther King, NAACP president Roy Wilkins, Vivian Malone, and Rosa Parks.

vented blacks from voting. That August, Congress passed the Voting Rights Act. It called for federal workers to register black voters. And it prohibited the use of the literacy test as a condition for voting. On August 6, 1965, President Johnson signed the Voting Rights Act into law.

As a result, the number of African-Americans registered to vote soared throughout the nation. By the end of 1965, a quarter of a million new black voters had been registered.

As African Americans gained political power, many ran for elected office. In 1968 Shirley Chisholm became the first

African American woman to win a seat in Congress. She was elected to the House of Representatives, from New York. In 1972 she ran for the Democratic nomination for president of the United States.

Still Work to be Done

Passage of federal legislation ensuring that African Americans would have the same rights as whites was the crowning achievement of the Civil Rights Movement. However, black activists did not stop once the laws were passed. They continued working to make sure that the rights of black Americans were protected.

The struggle for African American civil rights was long and painful. But by the late 1960s, Jim Crow was gone. The Civil Rights and Voting Rights Acts made discrimination illegal. Blacks in the South could vote without fear, and many more were registering. African Americans were running in local, state, and national races—and getting elected.

African-American civil rights activists had succeeded. But the struggle wasn't over. Racism and discrimination still existed in the United States, even if they were not as obvious as in the past. There was still work to be done. After the assassination of Martin Luther King Jr. in 1968, people like Jesse Jackson, Ralph Abernathy, Julian Bond, John Lewis, and others continued the struggle to ensure African-American civil rights.

Many people who took part in the Civil Rights Movements were overjoyed on January 20, 2009, when Barack Obama was inaugurated as the first African-American president of the

United States. However, serious problems remain for African Americans today. Many blacks are poor and are poorly educated. A high percentage of young African-American men are in prison, many on drug-related charges. And in recent years the deaths of young African Americans at the hands of police has sparked outrage among the black community.

 ## Text-Dependent Questions

1. What did the Supreme Court decide in *Plessy v. Ferguson* (1896)?
2. What act of civil disobedience sparked the Montgomery bus boycott?
3. What two major pieces of federal legislation in the 1960s provided equal rights to African Americans?

 ## Research Project

Using the Internet or your school library, do some research to answer the question, "Should racist speakers be denied a platform and censored?"

Some people believe that racist views should not be tolerated in a civilized society. Racist speeches can generate hatred and violence and are offensive to the majority of people in a country, so they should therefore be banned.

Others note that in the United States and other western democracies, it is an essential right of every person to have the freedom to speak their opinion, however unpleasant most members of the society find their views. They support the right to offensive speech, so long as it doesn't incite violence, and cite court cases that back up this principle.

Present your conclusion in a two-page report, providing examples from your research that support your answer.

How Does Racism Affect People?

Racism can affect people in many different ways. At its most common, racism involves distressing comments, jokes, and *stereotypes*. It can also prevent people from receiving fair access to jobs, education, and justice. At its most extreme, racism can lead to violence, murder, and entire countries or regions in which different races live apart.

Prejudice means to make up your mind about someone or something before holding all the facts—it literally means to pre-judge. Prejudice is based on ignorance and usually involves a negative judgement or conclusion being made against a person, group, or idea before knowing what that person, group, or idea is really like. A prejudiced person is likely to hold on to their views even when presented with the truth. Racially prejudiced people believe they know the character and attributes of

Activists lie on a street in Hollywood, California, pretending to be dead to dead, as a protest against police killings of unarmed African-American men in recent years.

people of color just because they can see their skin color.

Much racial prejudice is based on stereotypes. A stereotype is a fixed idea about what people are like. It tends to reduce whole groups of people to one characteristic—for example, all Mexicans are lazy or all Irish people are drunks. Even when the characteristic appears positive, such as "African Americans are good athletes," stereotypes remain insulting and unfair because they label and group together millions of people without considering them as individuals.

Racial stereotyping has occurred in all kinds of media including television, movies, and children's books. African-American men, for example, have been frequently portrayed as slow-witted and only good at physical work. In crime movies,

 Words to Understand in This Chapter

affirmative action—also known as positive discrimination, this is a policy adopted by a country or organization to attempt to make up for previous discrimination by favouring disadvantaged groups.

alienation—the act of making people feel alone, isolated and afraid.

immigrant—someone who moves to and settles in another country.

institutional racism—a modern term used to describe the processes inside an organization that can result in racial discrimination regardless of whether or not the members of the organization are racist.

prejudice—Negative feelings or attitudes towards a group of people not based on facts.

racial profiling—Targeting police investigations on the basis of a person's race or national origin.

stereotype—a widely held notion that all members of a particular racial, ethnic or social group have the same, often negative, characteristics.

Characteristics of Prejudice

In their studies of racism and race relations, experts have identified four characteristics of racial prejudice:

1. A feeling of superiority over members of a minority group.
2. A feeling that the minority is different and alien.
3. A feeling of rightful claim to power, privilege, or status.
4. A fear and suspicion that the minority wants to take the power, privilege, and status from the dominant group.

Eliminating racial stereotypes is an important element of defeating prejudice.

they were found on both good and bad sides, but until recently, they were often depicted as lowly henchmen taking orders from white bosses. Hispanic men are sometimes portrayed as lazy people who have come to America illegally. Asians are seen as hard-working to an extreme, not good at sports, and sneaky and conniving. Stereotyping in the media has been damaging because it limits how a person sees others and themselves, and helps to reinforce people's prejudices.

Spoken and written language can be used to cause offense. There are many obviously racist names, such as calling a black person "darkie" or a Chinese person "chink" that are used in this way. Other terms help reinforce stereotypes and may be used through ignorance, often with no spite intended. For example, many people in the United States refer to all people of Hispanic ethnicity that have certain racial characteristics (such as brown skin and dark hair) as "Mexicans" or as *immigrants*. However, many of these people were born in the United States—in fact, some Hispanics living in the southwestern states and California have family roots that date back to before these lands were part of the US. Also, they may come from many different countries in Central America or South America that have cultures that are very distinct from that of Mexico. By the same token, some people in Great Britain refer to all black or Asian people as immigrants, but most of Britain's blacks and Asians were born in the country.

Racial Discrimination

Discrimination involves treating one group less favorably than another. Racial discrimination denies members of one racial

Federal and state laws prohibit businesses and government agencies from discriminating against qualified job applicants due to their race, gender, or other characteristics.

group access to opportunities open to others: for example, when a college refuses entry to a black student with higher than average grades then admits a white student with poorer grades. Racial discrimination has hit many black and Asian peoples extremely hard by reducing or denying their access to the basic essentials of life, such as education, jobs and housing.

One study of employment agencies in Canada found that 94 percent admitted to discriminating against job seekers on the basis of skin color. In New Zealand, Maoris are three to four times more likely than whites to be unemployed. It is the same

The National Football League (NFL) established the Rooney Rule in 2003. It requires teams to interview racial minority candidates for head coaching and senior football operation jobs, though there is no quota or preference given to minorities in the hiring of candidates. People of color represented 10 percent of NFL head coaches before the Rooney Rule and 20 percent after.

for Aborigines in Australia, and only a little better for black people in many European countries. This only reinforces stereotypes and prejudice that certain racial groups are less likely to make good employees. People in jobs can also be discriminated against by being passed over for promotion, or by being given less favorable work conditions than white colleagues.

Many advocates claim that simply offering people equal chances to apply for jobs still discriminates against disadvantaged groups in society. They point out that marginalized people need to be given extra help to get a good education and learn useful skills. Otherwise, they will remain at a disadvantage in their search for work.

To ensure that everyone really does have an equal chance at a rewarding career, campaigners for equal opportunities have suggest *affirmative action* policies that favor people from disadvantaged groups. This might include increasing access to higher education or addressing disparities in job opportunities and pay for people of color, women, or any other group that suffers discrimination. It might also involve cultural, legal, and financial reforms to remove prejudice and inequality from society as a whole.

Affirmative action programs in the United States were inspired by the Civil Rights Movement. On March 6, 1961, President John F. Kennedy issued an executive order providing that government contractors "take affirmative action to ensure that applicants are employed, and employees are treated during employment, without regard to their race, creed, color, or national origin." Four years later, President Lyndon B. Johnson issued an executive order prohibiting employment discrimination based on race, color, religion, and national origin by organizations receiving federal contracts. Johnson's order said, "The contractor will take affirmative action to ensure that applicants are employed, and that employees are treated during employment, without regard to their race, color, religion, sex or national origin. Such action shall include, but not be limited to the following: employment, upgrading, demotion, or transfer; recruitment or recruitment advertising; layoff or termination;

rates of pay or other forms of compensation; and selection for training, including apprenticeship."

The intent of affirmative action programs is to reverse decades of discrimination and create a society in which people of all races enjoy equal social, political, and economic benefits. Campaigners argue that such policies should be judged not by their good intentions but by their practical results.

Not everyone supports the idea of affirmative action, however. Social conservatives tend to believe that affirmative action gives an unfair advantage to minorities, particularly in business and the workplace. They claim that under the free enterprise system in the United States, the employee or business that works hardest, brings the most talent to the job, and produces the best results is more likely to be rewarded. Under affirmative action, however, they believe that minorities don't have to do their best, or work their hardest, or possess the most talent, or bid the lowest to get a job.

Racial Harassment

Racial harassment involves racially motivated verbal abuse or physical violence against a person or their property. Racial harassment is very common in many countries and has proven to be hard to stamp out.

Racial harassment can range from racist comments, jokes, and graffiti to arson, violent attacks, and, in some cases, murder. In the United Kingdom, for example, there are an estimated 110,000 recorded instances of racial harassment every year. Many thousands more occur but go unreported.

Racial harassment at home, school, and work is often

Racial harassment is unwelcome behavior that happens to a person solely because of his or her race. Such behavior may violate state and federal laws related to discrimination in the workplace.

thought to be trivial, involving name-calling, racist jokes, petty theft, and vandalism. However, it is often persistent and repeated week-in, week-out for a long period of time. This

An English white supremacist walks with a "white pride" flag through the Exeter Respect Festival, an event intended to encourage diversity.

becomes incredibly distressing for its victims, shattering their confidence and leaving them feeling isolated, frightened, lonely, and an unwanted part of the community. This feeling of *alienation* can be increased when neighbors, classmates, and co-workers do nothing to stop it and offer little support.

Institutional Racism

Experts believe that just as individuals can be racist, so can certain institutions. The institution can be a business, a government, or an individual agency of a government such as the court system or the police force. *Institutional racism* can occur whether the members of the institution are racist or not. Its processes are what lead to racial discrimination and harassment.

In most countries today, the most powerful racial group controls the important state institutions—from schools and government to the army and police. Even if these institutions do not deliberately discriminate against any group in society and do not intend to be racist, they may still foster unequal treatment.

Studies have shown that African-American drivers are up to six times more likely than white drivers to be pulled over for traffic violations—a phenomenon that is ironically known as "driving while black" (DWB).

Racial profiling is not limited to African Americans; airport security checkpoints are more likely to identify travelers who are racially Arab or who are wearing traditional Muslim clothing for in-depth searches of their luggage and persons, due to concerns about Islamist terrorist attacks.

Institutional racism has been described as "policies and procedures within institutions that deny equal treatment to members of ethnic minority groups." Valerie Amos, formerly chief executive of the Equal Opportunities Commission, explains, "Historically, an environment has existed in which the favoring of individuals from certain groups, such as white men, has not been challenged because it is a norm. So, 'negative' discrimination, in favor of particular groups, became institutionalized."

Civil rights activists have long claimed that institutional racism exists. Examples include school tests tailored to white culture, or the higher percentage of white bosses leading to a higher percentage of white managers in corporations. However, an institution that is often accused of being opposed to minorities is the police force. Police forces all over the world have been accused both of institutional racism and of protecting racist members of their forces. In South Africa, there have been a number of instances of white police officers ignoring white racist attacks on black people.

In many countries, police target non-white people as suspects far more than whites—an action sometimes called *racial profiling.* Studies in the United States, the UK, and other white-majority countries have shown that black drivers are up to six times as likely as whites to be stopped and searched by the police.

In the United States there have been many protests in recent years about the killing of unarmed African Americans by police. The death of teenager Michael Brown in 2014 at the hands of a police officer in Ferguson, Missouri, led to riots and

Protesters participate in a parade on Martin Luther King Jr. Day, holding "Black Lives Matter" signs.

drew national attention to the issue. Thanks to the Twitter app, the hashtag #BlackLivesMatter became instantly popular. Protests and marches to draw attention to the issue have continued as other African Americans have been killed by police actions or died while in police custody, including Tamir Rice, Eric Harris, and Freddie Gray.

Studies indicate that most police officers accused of racism do not begin their careers as racists. Instead, the pervasive police culture, as well as their personal animosity toward lawbreakers, leads them to oversimplify the connection between race and crime. For example, a white police officer who may have grown up in a white, middle-class community where he experienced little crime suddenly finds himself assigned to a high-crime inner-city neighborhood populated by poor blacks and Hispanics. As a result, that officer may find himself concluding that blacks and Hispanics commit most crime.

Racism and Incarceration Rates

In most countries with a white majority, non-white people make up more of the prison population than their proportion

In February 2016, thousands of people demonstrated in Brooklyn after the conviction of police officer Peter Liang, who had accidentally shot and killed an unarmed African American man, Akai Gurley, two years earlier. African Americans wanted the officer to receive a prison sentence for the killing. Chinese Americans also demonstrated, complaining that although white officers had gotten off without prison sentences in similar cases, it appeared that an Asian officer was going to be punished.

Prisoners play basketball at the Dade County Correctional Facility in Florida. One study showed that one in six African American men have been imprisoned since 2001.

in society. For example, African-Americans comprised about 12.7 percent of the total US population, but they make up around 35 percent of prison inmates in 2014, the most recent year for which complete data is available, according to statistics from the US Department of Justice.

Some people feel that this is because non-whites are simply less trustworthy and prone to crime. Others think that in unequal societies with racial discrimination, non-whites are more likely to be poor and unemployed, and that these conditions tend to breed crime. A third point of view is that many non-white prisoners are victims of institutional racism in the police and legal system. This sees them investigated and brought to justice more vigorously than whites, handed longer or more frequent prison sentences and, in some cases, falsely accused and convicted of crimes.

 # Text-Dependent Questions

1. What is racial profiling?
2. What is institutional racism?

 # Research Project

Using the Internet or your school library, do some research to answer the question, "Is it ever acceptable to tell jokes that poke fun at someone's race?" Some commentators will point out that people make fun of those who wear glasses or are overweight. Jokes are meant in fun, and people must learn to be able to laugh at themselves. Others claim that the jokes tend to trivialize racism, which has caused much human misery. Racist jokes can also act as a way of promoting racial prejudice and damaging racial stereotypes. Present your conclusion in a two-page report, providing examples from your research that support your answer.

Fighting Back Against Racism

Racism occurs in many forms and there are equally as many ways to tackle it. Across the world there are hundreds of organizations, large and small, and thousands of individuals, all looking to combat racism and its effects.

Most racism is founded on prejudice, which itself is based on ignorance of other people. Racial awareness seeks to spread information about how all peoples are from the same race, and also how to understand and respect differences in history, culture and lifestyle. Books, movies, and classroom activities, along with public, school and workplace events, are all used to promote tolerance and understanding to help eliminate racial prejudice.

Some people believed that the election of Barack Obama as president of the United States in 2008 signaled the start of a period in which racism would no longer be an issue. By the end of the Obama presidency, however, it was clear that systemic racism remains a problem in American society.

Breaking stereotypes challenges lazy and prejudiced images of peoples and helps to promote the idea that people of all racial groups can be as successful as each other. It can also provide racial minorities with proof that success can be achieved even against the odds in a discriminating society. Early breakthroughs can provide a springboard for more to follow.

For example, in 1978, Viv Anderson—at the time one of only a handful of black professional soccer players in the United Kingdom—became the first to play for England. Today, around 20 percent of all professional footballers in Britain are black. In 1999 the organization Football Against Racism in Europe (FARE) was set up fight discrimination in European football leagues. FARE programs are supported by the Fédération Internationale de Football Association (FIFA), which oversees international soccer, as well as the Union of European Football Associations (UEFA).

In sports, the arts, and entertainment, non-white people who excel can become heroes and role models for people of all colors and ethnic backgrounds. Their successes help to break

 Words to Understand in This Chapter

felony—a crime, typically one involving violence, regarded as more serious than a misdemeanor, and usually punishable by imprisonment for more than one year or by death.

sweatshop—a factory or workshop, especially in the clothing industry, where manual workers are employed at very low wages for long hours and under poor conditions.

Soccer players from Argentina and Belgium teams pose for a photo with an anti-racism banner before a World Cup match in 2014.

down prejudice further, but there is still much work to be done and many organizations campaign to break stereotypes.

Although protests and campaigns can fail, and sometimes lead to violence, a number have contributed to lasting, positive change. This was the case in the US, with the civil rights movement of the 1960s pioneered by organizations such as the National Association for the Advancement of Colored People (NAACP) and the Congress Of Racial Equality (CORE) and individuals such as Dr. Martin Luther King, Jr. The civil rights movement used largely nonviolent tactics, such as boycotts of

There are people of all skin colors who support the Black Lives Matter movement.

certain services, powerful speeches, mass marches, and demonstrations. They achieved changes in law and society leading to more equal treatment for African Americans.

More recently, blacks have protested against the killings of people like Trayvon Martin, Michael Brown, Eric Garner, Tamir Rice, Eric Harris, Walter Scott, Jonathan Ferrell, Sandra Bland, Samuel DuBose, and Freddie Gray. The Black Lives

Matter movement has succeeded in bringing the issue of police attitudes toward African Americans to national attention. The candidates for president during the 2016 election were forced to take a position on issues that the concerned the Black Lives Matter movement.

In one event during the Democratic Party's primary, protesters confronted former president Bill Clinton, who was campaigning for his wife Hillary Clinton. The protester complained about a 1994 crime bill that Bill Clinton had supported and signed into law while president. The crime bill had resulted in hiring more than 100,000 additional police officers, included funds for new prison construction, and had banned

The Mississippi state flag flies over the capitol building in Jackson. Mississippi is the last state to include a Confederate symbol—in this case, the battle flag of the Confederacy—in its state flag. African Americans have protested against the display of Confederate flags on government buildings in southern states, because the flag is a symbol of a racist regime that wanted to preserve slavery.

For more than four decades, the Rev. Al Sharpton has been a prominent critic of systemic racism in American society.

certain firearms designated as assault weapons. But the bill had also included tougher minimum sentences for criminals, as well as a provision known as "three strikes and you're out" in which those criminals convicted of two serious *felonies* in federal court would receive a mandatory life sentence if convicted a third time. The provisions were blamed for an increase in the rate of incarceration in the United States that disproportionately affected African Americans. Clinton defended the crime bill, although he also acknowledged that the justice system treats many nonviolent criminals convicted on drug-related charges, many of whom are African Americans, too harshly.

Careful monitoring and international appeals cannot force any government to change its behavior, but they can bring unwelcome publicity, and encourage respect for human rights. Organizations like Amnesty International have supported such appeals. "The tragedies of Michael Brown [and others] impact all of us, everywhere, because everyone has the human right to life and to be safe in our communities, and to be free from discrimination and when these rights are not protected, our communities become locked in fear and polarized," said Amnesty International worker Muhammad Malik. "Mothers and fathers live in constant fear that what should ordinarily just be a walk in the park for their child might transform into a moment of brutal state violence. Communities lose faith in their judicial system and that lack of trust can lead to a sense of nihilism and depression that saps communities and undermines civic engagement. . . . Amnesty International supports an independent, impartial investigation of the death of Michael Brown and of the apparently heavy-handed tactics used by police in the aftermath of Michael's death."

There are many different targets for the large range of campaigns and protests that occur every year. Many campaigns seek to challenge and influence governments to change laws or to ask institutions, such as local councils and the police, to enforce laws more fairly. Other protests and campaigns are aimed at society in general, to make public a particular issue, such as cases of racial discrimination or severe cases of racial harassment. Some protests and campaigns target racists and racist groups by monitoring and highlighting their activities. Sometimes, there are direct protests outside meetings of racist groups. Other initiatives call for censorship to prevent racists from communicating their ideas through speeches, images, actions, or literature.

Laws to Combat Racism

Dr. Martin Luther King Jr. once said, "Judicial decrees may not change the heart, but they can restrain the heartless." By this, King meant that laws cannot remove prejudice; they can only make actions based on prejudice illegal. Since the 1960s, many non-white people in North America, Australasia, South Africa, and Europe have benefitted by legislation outlawing harassment, discrimination, and racially motivated violence. Yet, without education and ways of fighting prejudice, the problem of racism will remain, even if it is driven underground.

Some anti-racist laws have set up special bodies to help promote and enforce them. For example, in the UK, the Race Relations Act of 1976 set up the Commission for Racial Equality (CRE), which offers advice and support for victims of racial discrimination.

Affirmative action policies, usually backed by laws, are designed to counter discrimination against certain groups. In a fair society, religion, sex or skin color should have no bearing on the jobs, education, and other services a person is selected for or offered. This is the basis behind equal opportunities policies found in a number of countries. Although they have helped to remove some racial discrimination, equal opportunities schemes can sometimes be hard to police. It is difficult to prove that a person was rejected because of his or her skin color when a prejudiced employer or official gives other reasons for not hiring or admitting them.

Racism in Multicultural Societies

Many societies now claim to be multicultural, and this is usually assumed to be a good thing. Being multicultural means respecting different peoples' beliefs and traditions, giving them equal importance, and making sure that none of them oppresses the others. The aim is to promote tolerance and understanding, and to increase each community member's sense of security and self-confidence. However, equal opportunities campaigners have recently questioned whether multiculturalism really does help end racism and discrimination.

Some people argue that proponents of multiculturalism do not look deeply enough at the causes of racial discrimination. They contend that multicultural policies may allow for different ethnic groups living in the same region, but they end up divided into separate communities.

Families with the same ethnic background often live close together. At an individual level, this may bring benefits: people find it convenient to be near stores selling their preferred foods, clothes, literature, and music as well as have their own place of worship nearby. But for society as a whole, this can

 ## Can Racists Be Victims?

Some consider racists themselves to be victims of their own ignorance and prejudice, and of the persuasive methods used to recruit and keep people in racist groups. Racial awareness education has been aimed at children who have repeatedly made racist comments, and at young adults found guilty of racial harassment offenses. Some organizations try to assist adults wanting to leave extreme racist groups, a move that can be both difficult and dangerous. In Sweden, a government-backed initiative called Exit has helped more than eighty people to leave neo-Nazi groups safely and return to peaceful society.

A young African American holds up a sign he has made for a protest march against police brutality. The quote on his poster is a variation on the writings of James Baldwin, an African American writer whose novels and essays dealt with prejudice and the place of blacks in American society.

lead to problematic divisions and sometimes outbreaks of violence between rival groups who are intolerant of one another's way of life. These divisions between separate communities are often continued in the workplace, leading to a lack of career opportunities for some people and racial stereotyping.

Keeping people separate can also lead to abuses. For example, many Asian women work in Western countries as sewing-machinists and garment makers. They often perform this work in their own homes or in cramped factories known as *sweat-shops*. Many are exploited and underpaid because they are isolated and do not belong to trade unions or other organizations that might be able to protect them. Some do not speak the language and many have no knowledge of how to complain or assert their right to equal opportunities.

Success and Challenges

In Europe, the US, and many other parts of the world, men and women from ethnic minority groups are achieving great success. Their numbers are still relatively small, but they are growing.

Racial discrimination in institutions and in society as a whole leaves a wide "cultural divide" that members of minority groups have to cross if they want to achieve success. There is pressure to conform to certain expectations of speech, appearance, and behavior. African American tennis star Arthur Ashe complained of the stress he suffered from being "an ambassador" for the black community in the US. Everywhere he went, he felt it was his duty to act in a way that would prevent others from criticizing black people. He also admitted to toning down his regional accent, so it would be more "acceptable" to listeners.

The pressure to "fit in" can limit job opportunities. Skin color is one of the most obvious differences between people—even though it tells us nothing about a person's character or abilities. Even so, many institutions and companies are wary of hiring people from minority groups in case they do not "fit in." This is not logical, since the majority of non-white people in Europe and the US were born and educated in those countries, respectively.

Job applicants from ethnic minority groups can, of course, be better educated than applicants from the majority community. In 2013 in the United States, Asian students scored higher on average than white students on the ACT achievement test used in determining college admissions. But even where job applicants from minority groups are well educated, they can still find it difficult to gain job access due to unequal recruitment in many professions. For example, in the United States in 1987, people of color comprised only 12 percent of the total police force. While that number has risen to 27 percent in 2013, it is still below the 36.3 percent racial minority population in the United States.

Progress in the European Union

The EU has been called a "white man's club" in the past. Some member states classified people of non-white origin as "immigrants," even if they were born in these states. Until the year 2000, it had no laws protecting people from racial discrimination at work to match its laws on gender discrimination. The

Members of minority groups often encourage others to support businesses and enterprises run by other members of the group, such as this liquor store in South Central Los Angeles owned by an African-American.

Roma people, immigrants from northwest India who are often referred to as "Gypsies," have historically suffered violence and blatant discrimination in education and the workplace throughout the EU. Amnesty International reported in 2013 that there continues to be discrimination and violence against the Roma that was going unaddressed.

In 2000, the EU adopted the Race Equality Directive that prohibits discrimination based on race or ethnicity in employment, education, access to goods and services, housing, and health care. After the Race Equality Directive, concerted efforts by the EU have been made to improve equity among all races according to the following goals:

- Raise public awareness of anti-discrimination rights, with a focus on those most at risk, by involving employers and trade unions. Funding is provided to support such activities, along with a published a practical guide for victims of discrimination.
- Make reporting of discrimination for victims easier, by improving access to authorities.
- Ensure access to justice for those affected by discrimination with funds for training lawyers and non-profits representing victims of discrimination in how to apply equity law.
- Implement national strategies for Roma integration and protection with the general public.

Can Individuals Make a Difference?

Sometimes an issue like racism can seem so big and complex that individuals feel there is nothing they can do. This is simply untrue. Many individuals—from Dr. Martin Luther King, Jr. and Nelson Mandela to the schoolgirl or boy who reports racist bullying—have made an important difference. Every person can make a contribution to ridding the world of racism.

There are plenty of ways in which an individual can counter racism and its effects. On their own, a person can seek out information and learn more about racism and the issues that surround it. They can inform others about what they've learned and try to remove prejudice in their circle of friends. Many people have learned a lot from speaking to people who have been victims of different forms of racism.

An individual can also make a stand against any racist comments and actions they experience. Few antiracists think that confronting such behavior with violence is the answer, but challenging and reporting such behavior to teachers and parents can help. On many occasions, people find that when they make a stand against racism, friends, neighbors, co-workers, and classmates may follow.

Black filmmaker Spike Lee once commented, "When you're told every day for four hundred years that you're subhuman, when you rob people of self-worth, knowledge and history, there's nothing worse you can do."

Fighting Back Against Racism **91**

The Future of Racism

In many ways, racism should be yesterday's news. Scientists have proved that there are no separate species or sub-species of the human race and that the person you are does not depend on the color of your skin but on your upbringing; environment and experience. Yet, racism continues to exist in many forms in different parts of the world. Can it ever be overcome?

However, every day comes news and examples of racism in action. For example, the numbers of racial harassment cases reported in many European countries have stayed steady or even risen in the last five years. Does this mean that the work of individuals, pressure groups, and governments has been in vain? Not necessarily. Some increases in reported racist actions may be due to improvements in the way information is collected. For example, publicity drives in many countries have urged victims of racism to come forward with their experiences. Some of these victims are able to receive help. As a result, many people believe that a larger proportion of racist incidents are being reported than in the past.

Throughout the world there have been hundreds of small-scale success stories of individuals facing up to racist attitudes and, through education and experience, overcoming them. Using classroom discussions, activities and anti-racist videos and books, thousands of children have turned their back on racist bullying and name-calling. Knowledge and understanding of different peoples and cultures is increasing through improvements in transport and communication, and through the breaking of stereotypes via the media, arts and entertainment, politics, and other areas of society.

Countering all the different ways that racism occurs is an ongoing process, which makes it impossible to label as a success or failure so far. Certainly, some progress has been made, but clearly, more can still be done.

 ## Text-Dependent Questions

1. What black soccer player helped open the way to greater diversity in the sport in Britain and worldwide?
2. Why do African Americans protest against the Confederate flag?
3. What is the purpose of affirmative action laws?

 ## Research Project

Using the Internet or your school library, research the topic of fair hiring practices, and answer the following question: "Should companies have to interview at least one person from an underrepresented minority group for job openings?"

Some take the stance that the inequality in hiring practices, including granting interviews, has to be challenged. By requiring interviews of minorities, people of color will at least be able to make their case for the job, and bosses will have exposure to quality candidates from minority groups.

Others maintain that bosses should not be forced to interview anyone since it is their company they are running. If they have to interview minority candidates that they were not thinking about in the first place, they may just go through the motions, with no real difference in the end.

Write a two-page report, using data you have found in your research to support your conclusion, and present it to your class.

Key Equal Opportunities Laws in the United States

Racial, Gender, and Religious Discrimination

Brown v. Board of Education of Topeka 1954
Supreme Court declared separate schools for different races were inherently unequal and unconstitutional.

Civil Rights Act 1964
Banned discrimination on grounds of race, color, religion, sex or national origin in voting, public facilities, work, and education.

Civil Rights Act 1968
Prohibited discrimination due to race, religion, or national origin in the sale, rental, and financing of housing.

Civil Rights Act 1991
Provided for financial damages where people could prove job discrimination.

Gender Discrimination

Equal Pay Act 1963
Stated that men and women doing equal jobs should receive equal pay.

Title IX of the Education Amendments 1972
Outlawed discrimination on the basis of sex in any federally funded education program, including sports.

Pregnancy Discrimination Act 1978
Prohibited employment discrimination against female workers who were (or intended to become) pregnant.

Discrimination against People with Disabilities

Rehabilitation Act 1973
Banned discrimination in government jobs against qualified people with disabilities.

Section 504 of the Rehabilitation Act of 1973
Students with disabilities were allowed accommodations and modifications to coursework that addressed disabilities.

Education for All Handicapped Children Act 1975
Students with a disability were entitled to a free, appropriate public education and individualized education programs that addressed necessary areas of support

Americans with Disabilities Act 1990
Banned discrimination in all jobs against qualified people with disabilities.

Age Discrimination

Age Discrimination in Employment Act 1967
Protected people 40 years and older from job discrimination.

Age Discrimination Act 1975
Outlawed discrimination on the basis of age in programs and activities receiving federal financial assistance.

Organizations
to Contact

American Civil Rights Institute
P.O Box 188350
Sacramento, CA 95818
http://acri.org/

Amnesty International
5 Penn Plaza, 16th Floor
New York, NY 10001
http://www.amnestyusa.org/

**The Arc for People
with Intellectual and Developmental Disabilities**
1825 K Street, NW, Suite 1200
Washington, DC 20006
http://www.thearc.org/

Center for Equal Opportunity
7700 Leesburg Pike, Suite 231
Falls Church, VA 22043
http://www.ceousa.org

Center for Individual Rights
1233 20th Street NW, Suite 300
Washington, DC 20036
www.cir-usa.org

Equal Employment Opportunity Commission
Publications Distribution Center
P.O. Box 12549
Cincinnati, Ohio 45212-0549
www.eeoc.gov

**National Association for the Advancement
of Colored People (NAACP)**
4805 Mt. Hope Drive
Baltimore, MD 21215
www.naacp.org

National Organization for Women
1100 H Street NW, Suite 300
Washington, DC 20005
http://now.org/

US Commission on Civil Rights
1331 Pennsylvania Avenue, NW, Suite 1150
Washington, DC 20425
http://www.usccr.gov/

Series Glossary

apartheid—literally meaning "apartness," the political policies of the South African government from 1948 until the early 1990s designed to keep peoples segregated based on their color.

BCE and CE—alternatives to the traditional Western designation of calendar eras, which used the birth of Jesus as a dividing line. BCE stands for "Before the Common Era," and is equivalent to BC ("Before Christ"). Dates labeled CE, or "Common Era," are equivalent to *Anno Domini* (AD, or "the Year of Our Lord").

colony—a country or region ruled by another country.

democracy—a country in which the people can vote to choose those who govern them.

detention center—a place where people claiming asylum and refugee status are held while their case is investigated.

ethnic cleansing—an attempt to rid a country or region of a particular ethnic group. The term was first used to describe the attempt by Serb nationalists to rid Bosnia of Muslims.

house arrest—to be detained in your own home, rather than in prison, under the constant watch of police or other government forces, such as the army.

reformist—a person who wants to improve a country or an institution, such as the police force, by ridding it of abuses or faults.

republic—a country without a king or queen, such as the US.

United Nations—an international organization set up after the end of World War II to promote peace and co-operation throughout the world. Its predecessor was the League of Nations.

UN Security Council—the permanent committee of the United Nations that oversees its peacekeeping operations around the world.

World Bank—an international financial organization, connected to the United Nations. It is the largest source of financial aid to developing countries.

World War I—A war fought in Europe from 1914 to 1918, in which an alliance of nations that included Great Britain, France, Russia, Italy, and the United States defeated the alliance of Germany, Austria-Hungary, the Ottoman Empire, and Bulgaria.

World War II—A war fought in Europe, Africa, and Asia from 1939 to 1945, in which the Allied Powers (the United States, Great Britain, France, the Soviet Union, and China) worked together to defeat the Axis Powers (Germany, Italy, and Japan).

Further Reading

Alexander, Michelle. *The New Jim Crow: Mass Incarceration in the Age of Colorblindness.* New York: The New Press, 2010.

Branch, Taylor. *The King Years: Historic Moments in the Civil Rights Movement.* New York: Simon & Schuster, 2013.

Kendall, Gillian. *Nelson Mandela: A Life Inspired.* Boston: Wyatt North Publishing, 2014.

Internet Resources

www.amnesty.org/en/what-we-do/discrimination/
Amnesty International addresses discrimination
worldwide with news, information on issues,
initiatives for justice, and statistics.

http://databank.worldbank.org/data/home.aspx
Statistics on issues such as education, health, and
employment with demographics specific to race,
gender, and age.

www.dol.gov/dol/topic/discrimination/index.htm
The US Department of Labor provides statistics and
legal rights for people who face discrimination due to
race/ethnicity, gender, age, or disability.

www.eeoc.gov/laws/types/
The US Equal Employment Opportunities
Commission's site lists discrimination types and laws
protecting each group.

www.jimcrowhistory.org/history/creating.htm
This site links to several essays on American society
during the Jim Crow years. It also gives various
individual's perspectives on how Jim Crow affected
their lives.

www.loc.gov/exhibits/brown/
   Hosted by the Library of Congress, this website revisits
   the Brown v. Board of Education ruling. The site features photos of people and documents relating to the
   years before and after the 1954 order to desegregate
   public schools.

www.morethanabusride.org
   The website for the film *More Than a Bus Ride* provides background information on civil rights activist Jo
   Ann Robinson and the women plaintiffs in the class
   action lawsuit Browder v. Gayle.

www.pbs.org/wgbh/amex/eyesontheprize
   Based on the PBS American Experience television
   series *Eyes on the Prize: America's Civil Rights
   Movement 1954–1985*, this site links to profiles on people and documents from the time.

www.infoplease.com/spot/civilrightstimeline1.html
   US civil rights timeline with major historical events
   and laws from 1948 to present.

www.pbs.org/wnet/jimcrow
   This website provides background information on seg-
   regation in the United States and Jim Crow laws.
   Includes maps and activities.

www.rosaparks.org

This official website of the Rosa and Raymond Parks Institute for Self Development provides information on the institute and a detailed biography of Rosa Parks.

http://myloc.gov/Exhibitions/naacp/Pages/Default.aspx

The Library of Congress exhibition The NAACP: A Century in the Fight for Freedom provides information about the women and men who helped shape the organization during its first 100 years.

Index

Numbers in ***bold italics*** refer to captions.

National Association for the Advancement of Colored People (NAACP), 40, 42, 45, 48, 79
nationalism, 8, 15
Nazi party, 28, *29*
New Zealand, 27, 63
Niagara Movement, 40
Nixon, E.D., 48–49
nonviolent resistance, 45, 79–80
    See also civil disobedience

Obama, Barack, 56–57, *77*
Oliver Brown et al. v. the Board of Education of Topeka, Kansas. See Brown v. Board of Education

Parks, Rosa, 46, *47*, 48, *55*
Plessy v. Ferguson, *37, 42*
    See also segregation
police, 71, 72–73, 80–81, 83, *86*, 88
    killings, 57, *59*, 71–72, *73*, 80
Portugal, 20, 21–22
positive discrimination. *See* affirmative action
prejudice, 59–60, 61, 64, 77, 84
    See also racism
protests, *11*, 31–32, *59*, 72, *73*, 79–83, *86*

Race Equality Directive, 90
Race Relations Act of 1976 (UK), 84
races, 12, *14*, 16
    beliefs about, 9–13, 15, 24–26
    evolving concepts about, 24–28
    and physical characteristics, 11–12, 13, 15, 26–28, 88
racial awareness, 77, 85
racial discrimination, 62–66, 75, 87–88, 90
    and affirmative action, 60, 65–66, 84
    and Jim Crow laws, 35–38, 56

See also racism
racial harassment, 66–68, 85, 92
racial profiling, 60, *70*, 71
racism, 56–57
    and anti-Semitism, 20, 28
    and apartheid, 20, 29–33
    and colonialism, 19–25, 27
    and "cultural divide," 87–88
    definition of, 11–12, 15, 26
    and discrimination, 35–38, 56, 60, 62–66, 75, 84, 87–88, 90
    fighting back against, 16–17, 77–85, 87–88, *89*, 90–92
    future of, 92–93
    and incarceration rates, *38*, 73, *74*, 75, 82
    institutional, 60, 68–69, 71–73, 75
    and multiculturalism, 84–85, 87
    and prejudice, 59–60, 61, 64, 77, 84
    and racial harassment, 66–68, 85, 92
    and racial profiling, 60, *70*, 71
    and racists as victims, 85
    and segregation, 20, 27, 29–32, 35–38, 41–50, 51, 54, 56
    and stereotypes, *36*, 59, 60, *61*, 62, 64, 78–79
    victims of, 16–17
    See also slavery
Randolph, A. Philip, 41–42
religion, 15, 20, 25, 28
research projects, 17, 33, 57, 75, 93
Reynolds, Grant, 41
Rice, Tamir, 72, 80
Robertson, Carole, 51
Robinson, Jo Ann, 46–48
Roosevelt, Franklin D., 41

Schwerner, Michael, 53
Scott, Walter, 80

About the Author

Chuck Robinson lives in Louisiana with his wife Carol and their three children. A graduate of Dillard University, he currently teaches high school English. This is his first book for young people.